The Beginning
Of Wisdom

The Beginning Of Wisdom

Sermons For Pentecost
(Middle Third)
Cycle B First Lesson Texts

Sue Anne Steffey Morrow

CSS Publishing Company, Inc.
Lima, Ohio

THE BEGINNING OF WISDOM

Copyright © 1993 by
The CSS Publishing Company, Inc.
Lima, Ohio

Library of Congress Cataloging-in-Publication Data

Morrow, Sue Anne Steffey, 1949-
    The beginning of wisdom — sermons for Pentecost middle third / Sue Anne Steffey Morrow.
        p.   cm. — (Cycle B first lesson texts)
    ISBN 1-55673-614-2
    1. Wisdom — Biblical teaching — Sermons. 2. Bible. O.T. Former Prophets — Sermons. 3. Bible. O.T. Hagiographa — Sermons. 4. Pentecost season — Sermons. 5. Sermons, American. I. Title. II. Series.
    BS1455.M675   1993
252'.6—dc20   92-45764
                                                                                    CIP

9339 / ISBN 1-55673-614-2   PRINTED IN U.S.A.

In memory of my father,
Stewart Horner Steffey,
who first taught me the fear of the Lord.

Table Of Contents

Introduction

The rabbi rose from his desk. Reaching with two hands, he took the Hebrew Bible from the shelf. And as he balanced the large Bible on his lap he explained, "The Hebrew Bible is divided into three parts: the Torah, the five books of Moses; the prophets; and all that remains which we call the Writings. I don't know the Writings as well as I would like, but I'll try to help you. Now what was the text from Proverbs?"

"It's Proverbs 1:17," I replied. "Fear of the Lord is the beginning of wisdom."

"Ah, yes, here it is."

The rabbi put on his half glasses as he began to read the text. I noticed his eyes move from right to left as he read the Hebrew. An intense silence fell in the study as he studied the text. I sat still. I knew not to interrupt.

He looked up. He was silent for a moment before he spoke.

"There is a deep paradox within the text. The beginning of wisdom is to know there is much we will never understand, much that will always be mystery, to hold in awe.

"Awe is a way of living in relation to the mystery of all reality, to the numinous, the divine. The great Jewish theologian, Abraham Heschel has said, 'Awe is more than an emotion, it is a way of understanding. Awe is an act of insight into meaning greater than ourselves. Awe enables us to see intimations of the divine, to sense the ultimate in the common and the simple, to feel in the rush of the passing, the stillness of the Eternal.'

"But the paradox is deeper still. The Hebrew word for wisdom means skill. It means the capacity to discern, to judge. It means intelligence. In this definition of the word, wisdom is a human attribute. But throughout the Wisdom movement and the Wisdom literature in the scriptures, wisdom came to take on a deeper meaning. Wisdom came to mean our capacity to accept life's meaning and life's mystery, our capacity to understand our relation to the divine."

With a twinkle in his eye, the rabbi looked at me over his half glasses, "That's quite a little verse, quite a text."

Fear of the Lord is the beginning of wisdom. The Old Testament texts appointed for these Sundays in Pentecost reflect this ancient truth in one way or another. The first three texts taken from 2 Samuel tell the sad tale of David's turn from his fear of the Lord. Solomon personifies the ancient truth as he dreams for wisdom at the beginning of his reign, and builds a temple for the presence of the Lord. The text from the Song of Solomon reflects the wisdom of creative love. All three texts from the Book of Wisdom describe God as Wisdom; Wisdom as a holy teacher. Wisdom as a seeker of truth, wisdom as a virtuous woman. Esther's understanding of her relationship to God gives her courage and strength to stand up to King Xerxes.

"Fear of the Lord is the beginning of wisdom." As we sink ourselves into the writings of ancient Israel, and deepen our understanding of wisdom's ways, it is my hope that our knowledge will be increased, our respect for the integrity and beauty of the Hebrew scriptures will be deepened, and our awe for the one God be magnified.

Appreciation is due to Gloria Emerson, Elizabeth Duffy, Carol Cook and Helen Neinast, who read the text, to David Chewning who prepared the manuscript, and to the members of the congregation of the University Chapel who were eager to reflect on individual sermons after hearing them. Affection goes to my family, David, Jacob, Samuel and Ruth, who encourage me always along wisdom's path.

David's Turn
From Wisdom

Above my desk at home is a single pine shelf that holds a row of books, books which through the years have meant a whole world to me. You may have such a collection of such treasures, too, volumes by favorite writers of poetry, prose, narrative, non-fiction. Some of my books are so old that the covers are frayed and the pages yellowing. There is a volume I read for the first time last summer that is crisp and clean. Some have markers to note a beloved section or a poem I'd like to find with dispatch. Some are helpful in a direct manner, some reflective.

My line-up includes Strunk and White's *Elements of Style,* Willa Cather's *My Antonia,* St. Exupery's *The Little Prince.* William Zinnser's *Willie & Dwike* is the one I read last summer. I have Edna St. Vincent Millay's *Collected Poems*, in which the poetry reflects labor, love, loss. Her sonnet on grief moves me no matter how many times I reread it. "Time does not bring relief. You all have lied. Who told me time would ease me of my pain? I miss him in the beating of the rain." Two tales about the force of friendship are on the shelf, *Charlotte's Web* and *Fried Green Tomatoes.*

This little line of books is precious to me, I suppose because the books reflect, each in their own manner, my own life as

I am living it: memory, experience, sadness, hope. Together, they give me pleasure, spirit, perspective, spunk, revealing what it means to be human, underscoring that ultimately life is good. What volumes would you place in your collection? What books are most precious to you?

The Bible is, of course, such a collection, by favorite writers of prose, poetry, narrative, non-fiction. The Bible reflects memory, experience, sadness, hope. The Bible can give us pleasure, spirit, perspective, spunk, revealing what it means to be human, proclaiming that ultimately life is good. But distinct from the little collection of mine, the collection of books which make up the Bible tells, not only what it means to be human, but also what it means to be chosen — chosen by God, loved by God, led by God.

The section of the Bible appointed for the next four Sundays is a history book, or maybe it's an historical novel, or historiography. The writer is an exceptionally skilled historian, who is drafting an account of the final turbulent years of David's reign. The writer is looking back on David's long life and trying to explain what went wrong, why it all falls apart for David. David, whose love of God is intimately connected to his rise to power; David, who sings the psalms of praise to God like no other ever had; David, who embodies what it meant to be chosen. Why does it all unravel? What are the reasons for David ending his reign a beaten and a broken-hearted man?

The writer is also explaining why Solomon succeeds David to the throne of Israel, which is why scholars call this history the "Succession Narrative." The "Succession Narrative" runs from 2 Samuel 11 to 1 Kings 2. Most scholars date the narrative to the time of Solomon. Some scholars believe Solomon commissioned it. If so, then Solomon demonstrates his wisdom. For he chooses a writer who tells the gruesome tale of David's downfall, with precision and understanding, with integrity and a thread of hope. The narrative is a history, exquisitely written, revealing what it means to be human, our frailties and failures, as well as what it means to be chosen,

14

chosen by God, lead by God, loved by God. And finally the narrative observes how it is that God redeems us.

The text appointed for today is the introduction, the beginning of the end of David's reign. The text opens with David, King David of all Judah and Israel, rich and at the height of his power. It is spring: "The time when kings go out to battle." But David has sent Joab out to battle and remained in Jerusalem, so spring in the air means something besides battle for him.

David is taking a stroll on the roof of the royal residence, late in the afternoon of a leisurely day, when from his vantage point, his eyes chance to fall on an arresting and intriguing sight, a beautiful woman who is bathing. And David says to himself, "Mmm-Muhh" or words to that effect. Well, David makes a few quick inquiries and finds that she is Bath-Sheba, the wife of Uriah the Hittite. But spring is in the air. Uriah is away at battle. David is king and invites Bath-Sheba over and one thing leads to another, and that leads to a note that says, "Dear David, I am having a baby. Yours, Bath-Sheba."

Now I think you can see how this development could simply ruin David's arrangement. But after all, David isn't king for nothing. He does a little scheming and sends a letter off to Joab to have Uriah rotated back to Jerusalem for a little R & R. When Uriah arrives at the palace, King David calls him in to see how everything is with carrying on Holy Wars these days, and the food in camp and the weather.

But then David shifts the conversation a little. "Well, Uriah, you are here for R & R. I don't want to hold you all day. I know you're worn out from all that fighting, so why don't you go on home? You have relatives in Jerusalem? Oh, a wife? Well, bless my soul. You hurry home to her, and take tomorrow off, go ahead and take tomorrow off."

But, it turns out that Uriah was a real Eagle Scout and he refuses to break the rules of cleanliness and purity befitting a warrior in a Holy War. He rests and relaxes all night, but with the soldiers at the palace gate. He rests and relaxes, but not in the way that David envisions, not with Bath-Sheba.

15

Next David tries to break down Uriah's resolve with great food and good wine, but all this is to no avail, for Uriah never goes near Bath-Sheba, which makes it tough, impossible that Bath-Sheba is carrying Uriah's child. Finally, David sends Uriah back to General Joab with a note to see to it that Uriah is given such a dangerous assignment that he gets killed sooner or later, preferably sooner.

The tale is the beginning of the end for David, in one glance across the royal rooftop. David, who was the boy warrior and had faced the giant Philistine, Goliath with only five smooth stones and an unswerving faith in the name of the Lord of Hosts. David, who was made King over all of Israel, kept the covenant of the Lord. David, who was poet and musician par excellence, who composed and sang psalms of glory to the Lord, stunning songs like "The earth is the Lord's and the fullness thereof, the world and those who dwell therein. Who shall ascend to the hill of the Lord and who shall stand in God's holy place . . . the one who has clean hands and a pure heart . . . " (Psalm 24) But when David strolls across the royal rooftop and catches a glimpse of Bath-Sheba bathing, his heart is anything but pure, and he rubs his previously clean hands together in a gesture of urgency and desire and calls to his servants, "Who is that woman; get her for me." It is the beginning of the end for David, who forgets the word of the Lord that fear of the Lord is the beginning of wisdom and because of this "now the sword will not depart from his house."

And what does the text say about God? What does it mean to be chosen by God as David is? What does it mean to be loved by God as David is? What does it mean to be led by God as David was, at least until he took his very human stroll across the royal rooftop, and caught his very human glance of the beautiful Bath-Sheba bathing? How does God relate to those God chooses, loves and leads?

God is, in fact, strikingly absent throughout these opening verses of the Succession Narrative. God doesn't happen by, to place a cloud between David and Bath-Sheba, to save

16

David just in the nick of time. God doesn't intervene, not once, to save David from himself. David, who has offered so much and accomplished so much for God's chosen people of Israel. God doesn't come along to help David out, by somehow breaking down Uriah's soldierly resolve. Might not a merciful God have forgiven David's little lapse of good judgment into lust, lead Uriah to Bath-Sheba's side and saved everyone all the agonythat is to come?

No, at least not according to the writer of the Succession Narrative. This writer has observed the history and understood God's presence in a very different manner than miracle-maker or intervener. This writer observes the history and holds to a theology that is more like that of the wisdom tradition than it is of the earlier stories when God was parting the seas and dispensing manna. The wisdom tradition probes the human condition and God's subtle and mysterious relation to us. God acts in history, yes, but not directly. God acts in history, yes, but in a manner that always takes human freedom into account. God acts in history, yes, but more often than not in and through the human heart. God moves in a mysterious way, an unknowable way, God's wonders to perform.

Out on the royal rooftop in the spring of the year, the whole earth coming alive with the pleasures of propagation, the air filled with the lovely aromas of spring, of wisteria, and spicebush, bees buzzing as their work begins, the thrushes sweetly singing spring's song, David takes a stroll that becomes the beginning of the end.

So how do you imagine David, chosen by God, loved by God, led by God, feels in the last verse of today's text as he writes Joab in charge of the troops. "Set Uriah in the forefront of the hardest fighting and then draw back from him so that he may be struck down and die." How do you imagine David, King David, who sang the song, "The earth is the Lord's and the fullness thereof, the world and they who dwell therein?" How do you imagine he felt when he placed the letter to Joab in Uriah's hand?

How do you imagine David felt about Uriah, Bath-Sheba, himself, God? Is this command an act of desperation or of royal arrogance? Does David feel confused, guilty, angry, afraid of being found out, all of the above? And too ashamed to share any of this with God, who has been David's strength and shield all along?

Can God be trusted at the end as well as at the beginning? Will God be present to David through his sin? Will God redeem God's chosen one? Amen.

Nathan's Wise Parable

Last week we left David handing a note to Uriah to take to Joab. "Good luck, old chum, back to the front, God bless and all the best, glad you could have a little rest. Oh, by the way, could you deliver this note to Joab, a request for your commander from your king?" It was Uriah's own death sentence: Send Uriah to the forefront of the battle and then draw back from him, so that he might die.

Last week David left us wondering about his situation: to take Uriah's wife, Bath-Sheba, to discover that she is pregnant, to bring Uriah back so that Uriah might go to Bath-Sheba, and then to have his royal scheme thwarted by Uriah, who, as David's foil, will not break the law of purity befitting a soldier in a royal war. Uriah does not go near his wife. So David sends Uriah back to the front to be killed, with, he thinks, none the wiser.

News comes that Uriah is killed. Bath-Sheba makes her lamentations. David, as a good and compassionate king in the eyes of the people, takes in the poor, bereaved widow. David, as a generous king places her under royal patronage and Bath-Sheba becomes David's wife. It seems to be the end of the matter.

It is the end until the Lord sends Nathan to David. Nathan comes to David and says, "There were two men in a certain city, the one rich, the other poor. The rich man had very many flocks and herds. But the poor man had nothing but one little ewe lamb which he had bought. And he brought it up and it grew up with him and his children. It used to eat of his morsel and drink from his cup and lie in his bosom. It was like a child to him. Now there came a traveller to the rich man and he was unwilling to take one of his own flock or herd to prepare for the wayfarer who had come to him, so he took the poor man's lamb to prepare for the traveller.''

Then David's anger is greatly kindled and says to Nathan, "As the Lord lives, the one deserves to die, because he has no pity.''

And Nathan says to David, "You are the man.'' The truth must have stabbed David like a dagger into his heart: "You are the man.''

In all the commentaries on the text, throughout the midrash, the rabbis are unrelenting and like Nathan, hold David fully accountable. David had been chosen by God to lead the people of Israel in God's holiness. David knew God's justice and God's righteousness. David knew all the command-ments. David knew that once Israel was chosen by God, Is-rael was responsible to God, and his role as King of Israel made him especially responsible. In any other kingdom in the an-cient Near-East, it was well within the royal rights to take a subject's wife, but not in Israel. In any other kingdom in the ancient Near-East, it was well within the royal rights to have a subject led into battle for the slaughter of that subject. But not in Israel.

Israel was chosen by God to fulfill the purposes of God, to bind the words of God as a sign upon the hand and as front-lets on the eyes. Israel had been chosen by God to do what was right in the sight of the Lord; to love the Lord with all the heart and soul and might, to love the neighbor as self. And most especially, Israel was chosen to uphold the cause of the powerless, the fragile, the forgotten, to take the poor little lambs into their close keeping.

Nathan does not tell a parable about coveting, though David has coveted. Nathan does not tell a parable about adultery, though clearly David has committed it. Nathan doesn't even tell a parable about murder, though David was responsible for Uriah's death. No, when Nathan holds the mirror up to David, David recognizes himself in relation to God as one who has forgotten God's holy expectation, of God's compassion. David sees that he has had slain one who was cherished, was beloved. He had "despised the word of the Lord." He had done wrong. David looks at Nathan and confesses, "Behold, I have sinned against the Lord."

This section of scripture, that goes from 2 Samuel through 1 Kings 2, is called the Succession Narrative. It is a history of the final turbulent years of David's reign. The writer of the Succession Narrative is trying to interpret why it all falls apart for David. David, who as a child, slays the giant Philistine. Goliath, with five smooth stones and an unswerving faith in God, the Lord of hosts. David, who as King of Judah, triumphantly takes Jerusalem, and becomes King of all Israel. Why does it all fall apart for David, unravel in the most complicated and unseemly fashion? Why does it all fall apart, so that David suffers the death of three sons, the unnamed one born out of wedlock to Bath-Sheba, Amnon, and Absalom? Why does it all fall apart so that David ends his reign as King of Israel, a beaten and brokenhearted man, shivering, unable to get warm?

It falls apart because David forgets his responsibility to the covenant, because David forgets what it means to be chosen by God, led by God, loved by God. To be God's chosen is to be chosen by God to uphold the commandments, God's holy expectation of us all, and most especially to uphold the cause of those most vulnerable, the poor, the powerless, the little lambs. God is compassionate and God's judgment is upon us when we are not.

David actually pronounces God's judgment first. After Nathan recites the parable, David's anger is greatly kindled and David says, "As the Lord lives, this one deserves to die. Because he has done this thing, because he had no pity."

David knows the law. Then Nathan points out, "You are the one. Thus says the Lord, the God of Israel, I anointed you king, I rescued you, I gave you your house and your wives, and if that had been too little, I would have added much more. Why have you despised the word of the Lord, to do what is evil in God's sight? Now, therefore, the sword will never depart from your house, for you have despised me."

So, what if some present day prophet came to you with a parable, to what would the parable point? What if some present day prophet came and held up a mirror, what would you see? This passage can be more than a history for us. It can be a parable for us, a mirror for us. For we, like David, live in the covenant of God's holy expectation, the covenant that we love the Lord our God with all our heart and soul and might, and our neighbor as our self. And though few of us sit in seats of power like David, and few of us will turn from God in all the ways that David did, still we live in the covenant through all our days and all our nights. Like David we are chosen by God to love one another with all our heart, especially those who are lonely and frail, vulnerable and alone. Still we, like David, will fall short and find ourselves looking in the mirror sadly, but then face to face.

We need, like David, to confess, "Behold, I have sinned against the Lord." In the words of the ancient prayer, we need to confess "the sins that no one knows and the sins that everyone knows; the sins that are a burden to us and the sins that do not bother us because we have become used to them." I cannot look in the mirror for you but I can urge you to take a look, as if your life depended on it, for it does. We, like David, live in the covenant of God's holy expectation. God's judgment is upon us and God's grace is. Fear of the Lord is the beginning of wisdom.

Fear of the Lord is the beginning of wisdom. David confesses wisely, "I have sinned against the Lord." God's mercy prevails. David's life is spared. But God's judgment prevails also. And terrible the judgment appears to the writer of the Succession Narrative looking back on the history and trying to make sense of all of it: the death of the infant son born of the glance, the bloodshed and the violence, the wars and wars' ravages, the despair. David confesses, God's mercy and judgment prevail.

Then, tucked in the same chapter as the terrible judgment is the first hint of God's grace in the narrative. God's grace born to the same pair — David and Bath-Sheba. Then, David comforted his wife Bath-Sheba, and went in to her, and lay with her, and she bore a son, and David called his name Solomon. And the Lord loved Solomon. Fear of the Lord is the beginning of wisdom. Amen.

Absalom, Absalom

I was unprepared for the effect the Vietnam Veterans' Memorial would have on me. As we approached the low, polished black granite V-shaped wall, between the great memorials to Lincoln and Washington on the Mall. I felt the first wave of effect or shock and grief. I recognized a holy silence of all as we moved past the names, more than 58,000 of them, America's children whose lives were taken by the war in Vietnam. Our faces were reflected in the granite so as we begin to read the names Leroy Pierson, Jimmy Lee Plumley, Edmund Chester Polonski. We, the living, join with the dead. And there were bouquets of yellow rosebuds and a letter laminated to one who had died, Stephen. There were flags, of course, and loved ones rubbing a name. I was unprepared for the effect the memorial would have, and I caught up my own children's hands as I was caught by the agony of the war reflected in the wall. Why did we ever let all these young people die? These are the names of sons and daughters, those who once had dreams and delights, hopes and habits, treasured moments, a taste for life. Why were these children sent to fight? Why did they die? "Why" is the word that pierces the soul? As I held the hands of my own children, I remembered the words of one mother who said, "Yes, my son's name is on the wall and so is my heart." Every woman who comes to the site knows here are the names of the children of other women, and can for a little time imagine their despair. "Oh my son, Absalom, my son, Absalom, would that I had died instead of you. Absalom, my son, my son." Why did it happen?

It is, of course, the question which the writer of the Succession Narrative is asking through all the five texts appointed for these five Sundays in the middle of Pentecost. The writer is asking why, in God's name, did it all happen, all the agony, all the bloodshed, all the violence, all the grief. Why did it all fall apart for David, Israel's beloved king, chosen one of God? And speaking of God, where was God through it all?

We left David last week looking in the mirror of Nathan's parable, recognizing that he was the one who had sinned against the Lord. David's life is spared graciously but God's judgment is pronounced and secured. "The sword will never depart from your house."

And since last week, that judgment has played itself out. There has been rape and murder and rebellion, lust and bitterness, strife and dishonesty, cowardice, especially cowardice. It is a grim narrative and the writer spares us no details of the wickedness. Amnon rapes Tamar, his own half-sister, who is sister of Absalom. Amnon is David's firstborn, successor to the throne. David does nothing, though Tamar is his daughter. David does nothing, as if the rape never happened. So Absalom plots his revenge, the murder of Amnon. Absalom has a servant strike and kill Amnon when Amnon is drunk. Absalom then flees from the wrath of King David, his father. Absalom returns to Jerusalem, after a time, next in line, now, next in line for the throne, and impatient. Ambitious as he is, he plots a rebellion, an overthrow, conspirator against the king, son against the father. The night before the scene in today's text, David and Absalom, father and son, are encamped on opposite sides of the Jordan, readying themselves for the battle, readying themselves for the inevitable. It is poignant that David provides for his troops in such abundance: beds, basins, earthen vessels, barley meal, parched grain, beans and lentils, honey and curds, and sheep and cheese from the herd. David provides a lavish spread David cannot provide for his beloved Absalom ... on the eve before the final battle.

The sun rises. David orders Joab, his general and all the commanders, and all the troops and all the people: "Deal gently for my sake with the young man Absalom." The father asks that the son be spared. No amount of wickedness — not murder of a brother or rebellion of this rank can break up the love and the tenderness that David feels for his son and his successor, his heir to God's covenant. Nor can any amount of love and tenderness protect Absalom from himself, from the momentum of the rebellion he began, from the moment when he happens to meet the servants of David. And Absalom's mule goes under the thick branches of a great oak and Absalom's head catches on the great oak while the mule that was under him went on. Absalom is left hanging — though alive — until Joab takes three darts and thrusts them into the heart of Absalom, while he is still alive, hanging in the oak. And the armor bearers strike Absalom and kill him. "O my son, Absalom, Absalom, my son, my son, would that I have died instead of you, O Absalom, my son, my son." Joab wins the battle for David. Absalom is killed in the process. The writer is one step closer to finishing the Succession Narrative, but here the writer pauses so that we might grieve with David at the loss of this his third son, "Absalom, my son, my son."

Why in God's name did it all happen? What caused all the agony, the bloodshed, the violence, the grief, the order of life turned into chaos and disorder? Why did it all fall apart for David, Israel's beloved King, chosen one of God? Why does it so constantly fall apart? And why does it seem such a downward spiral ... evil and wickedness ... violence and war ... death and destruction ... human grief and human loss? It seems a complicated downward spiral, and there seems no stopping us ... no stopping us until we find ourselves at the angle of the War Memorial.

For the writer of the Succession Narrative, it is not complicated. The narrative is set in the context of our responsibility to God. The writer is relentless in the details and does not spare us. For the writer has a tale to tell, for God's sake, a direction in which to point us. The direction is to the covenant with God and our responsibility to it. All the sadness and the woe, all the grief and the loss are a result of David's sin, that David forgot that the fear of the Lord is the beginning of wisdom. God asks us to be compassionate always. God asks that we love God with all our heart and soul and might. God asks that we set love as a seal upon our hearts and we teach love diligently to our children. And we place ourselves in God's judgment when we do not. By the end of David's life, David sings a final song to the Lord, showing that he knows, he knows.

> *The Spirit of the Lord speaks by me*
> *The God of Israel has spoken*
> *The rock of Israel has said to me:*
> *When one rules justly over others*
> *ruling in the fear of God*
> *God dawns on them like morning light*
> *like the sun shining forth upon a cloudless*
> *morning.*
> *But godless men are all alike thorns*
> *that are thrown away*
> *for they can not be taken in hand*
> *and the one who touches them*
> *arms oneself with iron and a shaft of a spear*
> *and they are utterly consumed with fire.*

Observing the deaths of David's three sons, the infant, Amnon, and Absalom, standing by the names of all those killed in Vietnam, 58,000 of them, we pause, we agonize. We ask God for forgiveness and for wisdom. Amen.

The Dream
For Wisdom

In three swift verses, the succession is accomplished, finally. And David sleeps with his fathers and is buried in the city of David. Our prayer for David, companion in these past weeks, is that David sleeps, at last, in peace. For in those last years, David is so advanced in years, so old, that he cannot get warm. They cover him with clothes, but he does not get warm. They bring him a young maiden to lie beside him, but he does not get warm. I imagine David shivers in the knowledge of all that his life has taught him, the hard way. At the end of his life, David shivers in the knowledge that the fear of the Lord is the beginning of wisdom. Until Nathan and Bath-Sheba come to him.

They come to David to remind him of the promise for Solomon to succeed him. "Yes," David thinks to himself, shivering under a pile of covers. "Yes, that is the covenant, the promise, God is with me still. God forgives my indiscretion and my downfall: God has left me with Solomon." David warms a little with the recognition, son of his love of Bath-Sheba. Solomon is his successor, his son. Finally, David is calmed and warmed and as his time to die draws near, he calls Solomon to come to him, "Solomon, my son, I want to sum up what I know for you, as you begin, what looking back over my long life and reign has taught me. Hindsight is good vision, what looking back over my long life reveals to me, my son, is that fear of the Lord is the beginning of wisdom." Suddenly the shivering slows, David is calm as he shares what he knows, "Be strong, my son Solomon, and keep the charge of the Lord your God, walking in God's ways, keeping God's statutes as it is written in the law, that you, that you, my dear son, may prosper." And David sleeps with his fathers, and is buried in the city of David and Solomon sits upon the throne. The succession is accomplished.

The second portion of the scripture appointed for this Sunday in Pentecost legitimizes Solomon's succession to the throne. Moving over to the third chapter of First Kings, Solomon goes to Gideon to make a sacrifice as was the custom. At Gideon the Lord appears to Solomon in a dream. And God said, "Ask what I shall give you." Solomon answers, "You have shown great and steadfast love to your servant, my father, David, because David walked before you in faithfulness and righteousness and uprightness of heart and now, O God, I am in the place of David, and I am depending on you . . . I am only a little child. Or so it seems all of a sudden and I do not know if I am coming or going, and besides, I only got to the throne by the skin of my teeth. I only got to the throne because all of the other brothers knocked each other off and I was the only one left standing (except Adonijah, who was exalted but not for long). Then there is the subject of my mother, Bath-Sheba. She is rather infamous (not always admired). And there is the matter of the people of Israel you have chosen for me to lead. There are so many of them they cannot be counted. Who, who could govern them? Help! God! I am so scared! You ask what you can give? Please let's begin with an understanding mind to govern your people and an ability to discern good from evil."

At the very beginning of the reign, Solomon demonstrates his knowledge that fear of the Lord is the beginning of wisdom. Oh, maybe the source of this fear of the Lord is fear of the job of king. But never again will Israel know such

30

security, peace, well-being, affluence, as under Solomon's reign — 40 years of it. There is this extra little play on words as well since Solomon's name comes from the root of the Hebrew word shalo, "shalom" which means peace and wholeness and well-being. Solomon brings wisdom, peace and magnificence to Israel.

Fear of the Lord is the beginning of wisdom, peace, well-being. Solomon understands himself in this perspective, calls himself a servant of the Lord, four times during the dream. Solomon is a loyal vassal to all that God has asked in the covenant relation with their goal together set as the well-being of all God's people. When God said, "Ask what I shall give you." Solomon answers, "An understanding mind, and the ability to discern good from evil." This request is literally for a hearing heart. For the ancients, the heart is the center of the self and the soul. The heart is the place of thinking and feeling. The heart is the place for discipline and will. Solomon's request implies the desire for a reason that understands, a heart with the skill to listen, the ability to judge, an instinct for integrity. And it pleases the Lord that Solomon has asked it. The Lord grants what Solomon asks and adds to it.

The Hebrew word for wisdom — hokmah — distinguishes wisdom in three ways, all three of which are granted to Solomon. First and foremost, wisdom — hokmah — is the capacity to discern ... to reason ... especially good from evil. And it is the ability to make good judgments. Solomon demonstrates this capacity to discern soon after his dream at Gideon. Two harlots come before him both claiming to be the mother of an infant. Solomon calls for a sword, proposing to give one-half of the baby to each. The true mother responds, "Give her the child." The other harlot says, "Divide it." Solomon returns the child to its true mother and "All Israel heard of the judgment (hokmah) which the king rendered. They stood in awe of the king because they perceived the wisdom of God was in him, to render justice." Wisdom, hokmah, is the capacity to discern good from evil, the ability to judge.

The second meaning of wisdom — hokmah — is encyclopedic knowledge, used in practical matters such as government and administration. Wisdom is the knowledge of fact and the power to use that knowledge well and with skill. Solomon has such a knowledge. Solomon's wisdom in this manner is so wide and so deep that almost any spoken wisdom, from clever proverb to deep truth, is attributed to Solomon for generations.

Wisdom, hokmah, is also a secular asset, a kind of savoir faire, sophistication, savvy. This aspect of wisdom, Solomon has in good measure as well. His knowledge and capacity to discern, and his savvy, are all used to build Jerusalem's temple and Solomon's palace. Solomon designed courtyards and paths through Jerusalem. This particular aspect of wisdom reflects Solomon in all his glory.

Here at Solomon's beginning, during a dream at Gideon, Solomon asks for an understanding mind and the capacity to be a wise servant of the Lord, as king of Israel. And God is pleased with Solomon for making this request and God said to Solomon, "Because you have asked this and have not asked for long life or riches or the life of your enemies, but have asked for yourself understanding to discern what is right, behold I now do according to your word. Behold, I give you a wise and discerning mind, so that none like you has been before. I give you also what you have not asked, riches and honor. And if you walk in my ways, keeping my statutes and my commandments, then I will lengthen your days."

Threaded throughout these Old Testament texts appointed for these Sundays in Pentecost is the truth of what it means to be chosen by God as opposed to isolated and alienated. It means to seek to discern God's paths to distinguish between good and evil, to seek wisdom throughout our days. Amen.

The Temple
Of Wisdom

The text appointed for today describes the dedication of the Temple, the magnificent house that Solomon built for the name of the Lord. The Temple itself is something to behold, built of cedar and cypress overlaid with pure gold. It takes seven years altogether to complete the Temple, to finish all of the details; doors of olivewood with carved palms, open flowers, cherubim, an inner core of hewn stone and cedar beams. In the inner sanctum, the holy of holies where the ark would be placed, Solomon builds two cherubim of 10 cubits, approximately 180 inches, and those cherubim were overlaid with pure gold. When the Temple is finished, Solomon assembles the elders of Israel, and all the heads of the tribes and all the leaders of the ancestral houses of Israel. All is ready. The temple is filled with throngs of people. All those assembled hold their breath in holy expectation, as the priests bring forth the ark of the covenant. All assembled hold their breath in holy expectation as the priests place the ark of the Lord under the wingspread of cherubim 10 cubits wide. All assembled hold their breath in holy expectation wondering, would the Lord be pleased with the Temple as a dwelling place? The assembled also asked, "Would God make God's presence known?"

The priests come out of the holy place and the people's expectation is fulfilled, as a cloud fills the house of the Lord, "so that the priests could not stand to minister because of the cloud; for the glory of the Lord fills the house of the Lord." God's glory fills the Temple. God is present. God is known.

Scholars agree that 1 and 2 Kings is a history, a compilation of texts which includes the Succession Narrative, the Book of Acts of Solomon and the History of the Monarchs. Scholars agree that 1 and 2 Kings was written during the time of the exile, when the saving history of Israel seemed to be at a standstill. 1 and 2 Kings were written to support the people coping with defeat and despair, to strengthen the people of Israel in their obedience to the law and to point to Solomon's wisdom. 1 and 2 Kings were written to point to Solomon's relation to God as a model for the people, a model of someone who understood fear of the Lord is the beginning of wisdom.

This section of 1 Kings, Solomon's prayer of dedication for the Temple discloses Solomon's spirit of wisdom and understanding, spirit of counsel and might, spirit of knowledge and fear of the Lord, all qualities valued by the writer of 1 Kings. Solomon begins the prayer by acknowledging God's transcendence and imminence all in one breath. "There is no God like you in heaven above (as God is transcendent) keeping covenant and steadfast love for your servants who walk before you with all their heart (as God is imminent). Solomon's proclamation is quickly followed by Solomon's wisest question: "Will God indeed dwell upon the earth?" Is God present with us? How do we know?

It is the exiles' question, too, of course, is God present? How do we know? After Nebuchadnezzar and his troops descended upon them, ravaged Jerusalem, destroyed the Temple, killed the sons of the Israelites, left their daughters grieving widows, the Israelites questioned. After Nebuchadnezzar and his troops scattered the people, as a child scatters marbles across a school yard, scattered the people Israel into exile, the Israelites questioned: will God indeed dwell upon the earth?

It is our question, too, this question of God's presence. It comes from deep within the human soul and out of our experience ... as we see the faces of the starving in Somalia, as we read the statistics of those who are homeless in New York. Will God dwell upon the earth? Will God make God's presence known to us as we watch relationships break apart between those whom we love, or hear about a good friend who has discovered she is HIV positive? Will God indeed dwell upon the earth, will God become present to us? We ask the question as we struggle with our deepest longings, repeated patterns of pain, as we offer up our dearest hopes or face the fact of our mortality. It is our question, too, the question of God's presence.

The text which asks the question of God's presence also points us to the places where God may become present to us. The text points us first to the possibility of God's presence in the Temple, the possibility of God's presence in worship. Oh, much of the time for most of us, worship is a habit, a good habit, a time to sit quietly, to sing a few hymns, to pray a few prayers, to think about the week that is past and what lies ahead. But on occasion, even in worship, something will break through our habit, the Spirit of the living God. For example, one Sunday this past winter, I dropped into the late afternoon service of "Evensong," on my way home from work, weary from the day's routine. It just happened that the boys' choir was singing softly. The boys sang, "Tell out my soul, the greatness of the Lord, unnumbered blessings give my spirit voice, tender to me the promise of God's word, in God my Savior will my soul rejoice!" It was the sweetness of their voices and their song set against the harshness of experience, that suspended me. The song helped me to hold together the goodness and all that which is wrong. We are promised God's presence as we seek to worship God.

Next the ark of the covenant is brought into the Temple disclosing, as someone has said, "that God's moral claim is at the heart of God's being, and is the essence of God's presence." This is the truth which is threaded throughout the whole of 2 Samuel and 1 Kings: that, in a manner that remains mysterious, God is present when we live within the framework of God's intention for us. We place ourselves in jeopardy when we do not. An undergraduate writes from her summer service project, "The people here are modest and hard-working, filled with questions and with doubts, and our prayers in the morning are filled with the full gamut. Still we manage to serve over 100 people a hot lunch every day, collect clothes and distribute them, raise funds to keep our doors open, laugh a little, hold each other close. God is present at the settlement house for those who seek to live out God's will."

Finally, the text points us to the reality that God is numinous and mysterious, awesome and aweful. Solomon knows that the highest heaven can not contain God, much less the house that Solomon has built, that God's power and God's presence is beyond human understanding. One midnight this past summer, in the little stretch of north Canadian woods where my family vacations, my mother, brother, sister and I had gone down to the dock for a midnight swim in the bay. When all of a sudden the sky lit up in a manner that defies description, as if some wild someone was flashing a cosmic strobe throughout the sky. The once brilliant stars were lost to the brilliance of this other display, streaks of light, colored in green and rose and gold, streaks moving in great circular swishes and gorgeous patterns. My brother ran to rouse sleeping husbands and children, but he needn't have hurried for these northern lights lasted for hours and were a sensation. We watched spellbound until the lights had finished and returned the sky to a heaven full of brilliant stars.

We spent much of the next week wondering about the northern lights, researching what had caused them, blowing the dust off star books in the lodge library to try to discover what had caused such a sensational display. In my grandmother's 89 summers, she could not remember northern lights like we had seen. We did not know, we were not sure. But of one thing I was certain, my understanding of God was radically altered. To see the night sky explode with color and movement and flashes of light flooding our gaze, is to know God as fluid, and changing; breathtaking in God's dynamic strength, awesome, aweful.

We may experience God's elusive presence in our worship, in our striving to live out a moral life which is God's intention for us, in our accepting God as Other, high above the heavens. Amen.

Solomon's
Song Of Love

It was summer heaven on the mountain. We woke to the song of thrushes and rose to watch the fog moving and lifting through the valley. We lit a little summer fire, with doors and windows opened wide. The coffee began to perk, the children to stir. We plotted and planned summer adventures: a creek hike in search of salamanders, a picnic at the top of the mountain, carpeted with ferns, where the laurel was at its peak. And yes, I got a terrific case of poison ivy, picking black-eyed Susans for the grandmother's return. It was summer heaven on the mountain, a blessing of creation, abundant, full.

This is the song which Solomon sings, the goodness of creation, in the portion of the Song Of Solomon appointed for this morning. "For lo, the winter is past, the rain is over and gone, the flowers appear on the earth, the time of the singing of birds is come and the voice of the turtledove is heard in our land, the fig tree puts forth its fruit and the vines are in blossom, they put forth fragrance."

This is a song of the goodness of nature. Someone has said, in fact, that it is the most beautiful song to nature in the Old Testament. And it is a song that each of us has sung at times in our lives, I hope, when we are filled with the beauty of the world and the wonder of the pattern of nature. The goodness of creation is reflected on an autumn afternoon, when the trees are dripping with color, like an artist's autumn palette all crimson and orange and gold, and the world itself seems an abundant place. The goodness of creation is reflected when you rise on a winter morning and the new moon is hanging in the winter sky, two planets shine brightly beside the crescent as the sun edges its way up toward the horizon. It is cold and clear and breathtakingly beautiful. It is cold, better get the newspaper and get back inside. The goodness of creation is reflected in the seasons, spring and summer, autumn and winter. There is a pattern to the created order and it is good. "For lo, the winter is past."

But the Song is not simply a song to the goodness and beauty of creation, a simple song to spring arriving. No, the creation song is only background music to the main tune of the Song Of Solomon, which is this song of love, the song of two lovers: "the voice of my beloved, look, he comes leaping over the mountains, bounding over the hills," "my beloved is like a gazelle, or a young stag," "my lover is mine and I am his, who browses among the lilies," "catch us the foxes, the little foxes that damage the vineyards when the vineyards are in bloom."

The Song Of Solomon is, in fact, a collection of 25 lyric poems, love poems, poems written to the glories of eros, human sexual love in all of its fullness. Take a moment this afternoon, if you have a moment after chapel, maybe after lunch, to read the entire Song, but be prepared, the room you are reading in may get a little steamy. For the Song Of Solomon is a clear melody to sexual love. The song says that such love should be sought after and treasured when found. These poems are an unapologetic depiction of two lovers and all that they share, their tenderness, intimacy, longing, illusion, mutual esteem of and desire for each other's bodies. The Song Of Solomon is a song sung to the mysterious and glorious dimensions of human sexual love.

Scholars have most often placed the Song in the body of biblical wisdom literature. I imagine it is placed there because

Solomon's name is attached to it. Different from the texts of the Bible which deal with the past, the histories, and the texts which deal with the future, the prophets, different from the texts that describe the liturgies and worship of God, as most of the psalms do, wisdom literature deals with the present, the here and the now. Wisdom literature probes the present and asks questions of the meaning of life and of death, of suffering and of time. Wisdom asks us to be realistic for God's sake: to stand up to God in the midst of terrible suffering, as Job does; to be terribly honest about life's limitations and the fact of death, as Ecclesiastes the Teacher is. Wisdom keeps us on the straight and narrow path as the collection of Proverbs attempts to do. And integral to wisdom's search for understanding is wisdom's relation to the divine. Biblical wisdom literature presupposes the existence of God, understands God to be the Source of wisdom, wisdom's fount. God is even personified as wisdom. Wisdom's theology may be subtle, may be sophisticated, may be radical, but there is a theology, nonetheless, a study of God and God's intention for us in the wisdom corpus.

But in the Song of Solomon, God is not mentioned. In the Song, God is not mentioned, no, not once. And for this reason and because the Song Of Solomon does not ask questions or glean for wisdom, I line myself up with the scholars who place the Song of Solomon in another category altogether, a category of its own. The Song Of Solomon simply sings the song of love. It is a song sung to the goodness of all that is created, as something desirable, in and of itself, to the goodness of creation and human sexual love.

Listen to parts of the poems, to the wonderful exchange, the metaphors, illusions, the coyness in the lover's voices:

O that you might kiss me with the kisses of your mouth, for your love is better than wine.

Behold, you are beautiful, my love, behold you are beautiful.

Your shoots are an orchard with all the choicest nard, and saffron, calamus and cinnamon.

How sweet is your love, my sister my bride, you have ravished my heart with a glance of your eyes.

I arose to open to my beloved and my hands dripped with myrrh, and my fingers with liquid myrrh.

My beloved has gone down to his garden to the bed of spices, to pasture his flock in the garden, to gather lilies ...

Eat O friends and drink, drink deeply of lovers.

God knows we know how complicated the good gift of human sexual love is. As a church, as communities of faith, we strive to live with the most difficult questions of human sexuality — what does it mean to be faithful? What does it mean to be responsible? How can we educate our children to be intelligent, thoughtful, careful, respectful? We strive to live with the difficult questions this century has introduced, the questions of choice and freedom, questions of protection and responsibility. God knows we know how quickly the power and attraction of human sexuality can be misused and abused, how quickly our longing for intimacy gets confused with our need for release or our own need for security. Our questions and concerns help us to articulate ethics and guidelines for safety in a world where sex is often a dangerous game. And all of our questions and struggles and concerns and guidelines and ethics and models for behavior as individuals and in community are an essential part of our lives as Christians, as faithful Christians and responsible Christians.

But on this Sunday, when the sweetness of summer is still in the air, and the second growth of raspberries ripen to their full flavor on the bushes, on this Sunday, when the summer roses cast an aroma that catches us up in the subtlety of their smell, on this Sunday we are called by this text to claim the goodness of all that is created and especially claim the goodness of our sexuality, the beauty of our bodies and the pleasure that the gift of love and loving gives to us: "My beloved is mine and I am his. He pastures his flock among the lilies. Turn, my beloved, like a gazelle, or a young stag upon the mountains." Amen.

Wisdom
In A Proverb

What is a proverb? It is a short, popular saying, usually of unknown or ancient origin, that expresses some commonplace truth or useful thought. What is a proverb? It is a pithy saying characterized by "its shortness, its sense, its salt." What is a proverb? It is an adage, easily remembered, that forms either an observation or a judgment. What is a proverb? It is a maxim that expresses simply and concretely a truth based on common sense and human experience. Many of our grandmothers had more proverbs up their sleeves than you could shake a stick at, so just for the fun of it, let's take a few moments and share favorite proverbs. Let's see how many we can name for the pleasure of it:

You can lead a horse to water, but you can't make it drink.
Birds of a feather flock together.
A stitch in time, saves nine.
Chickens come home to roost.
What goes around, comes around.
A new broom sweeps clean.
Out of sight, out of mind.
A rolling stone gathers no moss.
Don't look a gift horse in the mouth.
Don't borrow trouble.

Dead men tell no tales.

Angels go where wise men fear to tread.

From deep within the folk wisdom, we find simple truths that are stated so aptly, that they become proverbs. These are insights into human behavior, norms, rules, right values, due proportions, patterns, that become proverbs when they are spoken again and again and again to illustrate a point, clinch an argument, lend authority to some admonition or provide a warning. Proverbs also have a teaching function. They are a great way to transmit knowledge, and teaching was the intention of those who compiled and edited the collection that we know as The Book Of Proverbs.

The Book Of Proverbs is a sourcebook of instructional material meant for use in school or private study, directed at young people, a sourcebook for the cultivation of personal morality and practical wisdom. The Book Of Proverbs is an ancient "how to" book, that became a bestseller and was included in the canon. Now I do not know how many of you have ever read the Book Of Proverbs, but I will tell you (and not as a confession, but rather as a matter of fact) that I had not read Proverbs until recently, until I began to study the texts from Proverbs appointed for the next three Sundays. Someone has said, that apart from Leviticus, Proverbs is the least read portion of the scriptures. But the value of the lectionary is that it leads a preacher and a congregation to parts of the scriptures that we would not choose for ourselves. So it is with Proverbs.

Proverbs is part of the wisdom literature of the Hebrew scriptures which includes Job, Ecclesiastes, Esther, and some would say the Song Of Solomon. The wisdom literature sought to probe the human experience and attempt to make sense of it, probe the human experience in its fullness and find meaning, direction, clues to righteousness.

The wisdom movement was international. The sages sought wisdom from the surrounding civilizations. Hebrew wisdom literature has much in common with the literature of the Edomites and those from Phoenicia, the Egyptians and those from Mesopotamia.

There is respect for the religions of other civilizations, but wisdom literature is set in a distinct frame. For the Hebrew sages, "fear of the Lord is the beginning of wisdom." As the sages gleaned human experience it is always in relation to God. The relation is defined by fear, respect, awe, understanding of Yahweh's power and presence and will. Yahweh's commandments and intention and justice is the beginning of human wisdom and knowledge and the capacity to lead a life that is righteous and good.

Proverbs itself falls into three sections. Happily, we have one text from each, though for reasons I can not determine, we begin with a text from the middle of Proverbs. Today's text is from the sayings of Solomon and the sayings of the sages. Solomon was the patron saint of the sages and the wisdom movement; Solomon, who was remembered for his intelligence and shrewdness, good sense, sound judgment, moral understanding, wisdom. The collection of proverbs under Solomon's name is the major portion of the Book Of Proverbs and gives it its distinct tone: proverbs that teach how the good life is to be achieved.

Yet there is difficulty with this collection of Proverbs in relation to our search for wisdom and understanding. Proverbs are individual sayings which really should be considered separately. Someone has said, "To read through the sayings is like trying to have a conversation with someone who always replies with one liners. The first few may serve to amuse, but after a dozen or so, it gets boring." One stops listening. One stops reading. Proverbs is not designed for continuous reading. Even our short text for today is a case in point:

A good name is to be chosen rather than great riches, and favor is better than silver and gold.

The rich and the poor have this in common: the Lord is maker of them all.

Whoever sows injustice will reap calamity, and the rod of anger will fall.

Are you reaching the saturation point yet?

Those who are generous are blessed, for they share their bread with the poor.

45

Do not rob the poor because they are poor, or crush the afflicted at the gate; for the Lord pleads their cause and despoils the lives of those who despoil them.

So how are we to approach a text from the sayings of Solomon, the middle section of Proverbs? We approach Proverbs carefully, with open minds but also with our eyebrows raised in suspicion, with our hearts eager but also with a grain of salt. As we search for wisdom in our experience, as we seek to discover ourselves what it means to be human, we recognize:

that life is filled with contradictions, and so is Proverbs;

that life is filled with ambiguity and so is Proverbs;

that life is sometimes exaggerated, and so is Proverbs;

that life is neither simple or simplistic and when Proverbs appear to be, it's best to remain flexible, for the proverb will soon be deepened or be qualified or discounted.

There are moments of almost slapstick humor in Proverbs and there are moments of holiness and it's important to understand which is which.

So I suggest that we approach Proverbs one at a time: dwell on one proverb, consider it, think about it, expand it in your view, relate it to your experience, to those who you know, argue with the proverb, find its loophole, probe it to see if there is truth or wisdom to be found.

For instance, let's consider "those who are generous are blessed, for they share their bread with the poor." Take a moment now to think of people you know who are generous. Think of particular acts of generosity; (add your own here) I am thinking about a time when a friend came with a bunch of sweet peas just when I needed them and about a gift to the Student Volunteers Council that surprised us completely. Imagine the pleasure it gives people to be able to be generous, to have the freedom and the time to be generous. Think also of the strength it sometimes takes, and the discipline. Take a moment to think of someone in your life who is generous while I tell you about a colleague whose family includes a 51-year-old brother-in-law who lives with cerebral palsy and is wheelchair-bound. All that my colleague does at home is

46

defined by this family member, whether they can go out to dinner or to a movie or where or when they might take some time away. It doesn't seem extraordinary to her or to her children. "Those who are generous are blessed."

Another example is a neighbor I know who always spends her birthday and Christmas in a soup kitchen distributing food. This is a small sign of her generosity which includes sweeps of generosity to godchildren, constant commitment to a Lutheran church on the lower East Side of New York, to Palestinian refugees who need financial as well as emotional help. As I consider those who are generous that I know, I recognize that generosity is a way of being, not an occasional gesture and the way of being means sacrifice and it means blessing. "Those who are generous are blessed," for they share what they have — their selves and their souls. So read the Book Of Proverbs as you would a cookbook. Dwell with one proverb, as we have done, as you would one recipe. Spend time with it, study it, "bake it" and see how it comes out. Amen.

God
As Wisdom

If someone like me were to ask someone like you, "How do you imagine God?" what would you answer? What is the first word that comes to your mind when I say God? Creator? Love? Mother? Friend? Jesus? Help? Shepherd? Defender? How do you imagine God? When you are praying, how do you experience God? As strength? As light? As comfort? All-encompassing? How do you imagine God? Is God someone with a large protective shoulder to lean on, when you are more than a little scared? Is God a strong warrior who will help you fight your way through hard times? Does your image of God give God great majesty, high and lifted up, like Christ enthroned in our Great South Window? Or is your image of God close and intimate, embracing, soothing and accepting you through it all? Some people imagine God as a place and a shelter, a cave or a river, a mountain or a harbor. Some imagine God alongside them seeking justice, among us in acts of compassion. If someone like me were to ask someone like you, "How do you imagine God." How would you answer?

This is not an easy question to answer for our images of God are often formed unconsciously. They are formed by the lullabies your mother sings, or what your father reads to you when you are still at his knee. Your image of God may be

49

formed by your grandmother, a strong disciplinarian, you still remember, by Sunday school where you had to wear scratchy grey flannels and which you found an incredible bore, or by singing "The National Anthem" at the baseball game. Our images of God are created by bits and pieces of human experience, the good and the hard, whether the world welcomes us or seems a hostile place, the shocks we experience, the hard-knocks, the care we receive and the care we do not. Our images of God are a complex mix of unconscious material and human experience. They reflect life's most intimate moments and our hearts' deepest longings, so our images of God are often difficult to determine, to describe, to talk about.

Now I'd like to push us a little further. How has your image of God changed through the years, or has it? Sometimes, our images remain the same as the ones we receive when we are children especially if those images work, are ones that give us comfort and sustain us. It is the old proverb, "If it isn't broke, don't fix it." At other times, we have an experience that forces us to question our image of God, to question it and change it. A friend who lives in South Florida has organized hurricane relief in his area. The other night on the phone he remarked cryptically, "I don't get God, Sue Anne. This is so unfair! The people who were struck the worst by Hurricane Andrew are the ones who can afford it least. We're having trouble reaching those who are in greatest need, especially the illegal aliens, Haitians, a lot of them in Homestead. They are frightened to come forward to get food and be led to shelter. They are frightened for themselves and their families. Isn't it enough that they had to flee from the Haitian regime? Where is God for them? Isn't living through Andrew enough, for God's sake, that now they have to be frightened of help?''

Has your image of God changed over the years? The moment my own father died, God as father died for me. I didn't know it then, at least not consciously. But God as Father, giver of life, giver of love, God full of passion and pleasure, goodness and adventure, that God died when my own father did.

God as father was, for me, projection, and if I couldn't have my real father, I certainly did not want some heavenly one. And in that father God's stead came Silence at first, capital S, Silence, dark, holy, vast, God as Silence. How has your image of God changed over the years through your life's experience?

Our images of God reflect who we are, where we are, and how we are. We are made in God's own image, are we not? But they also may change through study and reflection. So, on occasion, it is valuable to set time aside to consider how it is we imagine God and to give ourselves the opportunity to study and to reflect how it is God relates to us, and whether there are ways to stretch our imagination of God so that our relation to God may be deepened or strengthened, which leads me to the text appointed for today that describes God as Wisdom.

There have been a number of times in recent weeks when I have called upon God and what I thought of as God's wisdom. Balancing my checkbook after vacation, "O God, help me to be smart and wise, give me humor and perspective as I straighten out this mess, anticipate the vacation Visa bill, and keep this family from financial ruin." Disciplining an obstreperous child, wanting to slam doors, kick and scream back, (bad behavior is contagious, have you ever noticed that?) I took a deep breath and called on God to give me understanding and wisdom, the long view. Saying good-bye to a treasured colleague of many years, standing by his moving van, I asked God for the right words to sum up 11 years together, wisdom in a sentence or a moment. Then as the tears began to stream down my cheeks, I said, "I'm not much good at this part so let me just say thanks and run."

In each of these circumstances, I was pleading, hoping, praying for wisdom. I was praying for good judgment, the capacity for understanding and direction.

But that wisdom, what I call the "gentle, kind and wise, wisdom" is very different from how God is imagined as wisdom in the Hebrew Scriptures, different from God as wisdom

51

as she is portrayed in the texts for this morning. Wisdom as portrayed in the Book Of Proverbs as different an image of God as I can imagine. Let's take a look at this image to see what we might see, to learn what we might learn.

Wisdom is, to start with, feminine, the Hebrew feminine, and wisdom has a life of her own. She is strong and she is proud. And she would be impatient with my pathetic pleas for help. Wisdom cries out in the street and on the square. She shouts, "how long, O simple ones, will you be simple?" "I will laugh at your calamity." "I will mock when pain strikes you, because I have called you and you refused, because you have ignored all my counsel." Wisdom, as she is presented in the Bible, is a serious teacher, strict and harsh and she is not into second chances or forgiveness. She demands that we pay attention. She proclaims "all the words of my mouth are righteous, there is nothing twisted or crooked in them." Wisdom seems not only proud, but here she appears arrogant. Is this someone you want as a professor? Is this someone to whom you would grant tenure?

Still it is hard to turn away from her. She is intelligent, holy, unique, manifold. Even though she is sometimes angry, she is incisive, irresistible and active. She is penetrating, for she is pure, she is subtle.

Wisdom is a woman who knows her value and wants us to know her value, too. She is committed to the task of learning constantly and to seek understanding of the world in which we live. She is out on the streets and calls us to think, think hard about what is happening in Homestead and in Yugoslavia, in Trenton and in Somalia. She is relentless in her expectations, demanding, unwavering in her standards for perfection. Then, she promises that disciplined learning and attention will be rewarded.

"The beginning of wisdom is this: Get wisdom and whatever you get, get insight. Prize her highly and she will exalt you. She will honor you if you embrace her. She will place on your head a fair garland. Get wisdom. Get insight. Do not forsake her and she will keep you. Love her and she will guard you."

In the mid '70s there was a television program called "The Paper Chase," about life at the Harvard Law School which starred John Houseman as the gruff/tender quintessential Professor Kingsfield. Many clergy had professors like Kingsfield in seminary. The syllabi for these professors' courses always overwhelmed students with their "completeness." Reading assignments were lengthy. Writing assignments were weekly. He shot questions at us during precepts, one right after the other. Preaching was a daunting task. We knew we'd never have such a harsh critic again, yet we all took his courses one after another, for as crusty and commanding as he was, we knew his heart and soul as well as his mind was in his teaching. "It is the gospel that is at stake here and you are going to know it!" God as wisdom.

If someone like me were to ask someone like you, "How do you imagine God?" how would you answer? Now, I hope we might consider wisdom as a worthy image of God for us. She is complex, independent and invaluable, illusive, coy, sometimes difficult in her demands. Yet the scriptures proclaim that she is at the heart of the learning process. With her strong sense of self and commanding sense of direction and discipline, she is at the heart of the creative process. And the promise in the text is that, commanding as she is when she tells us to fear the Lord, as she shouts at us, shakes her fist and calls us to account, those who listen to her will live securely, without dread, and will live at ease. Will you?

Who Can Find
A Virtuous Woman?

School girls we were, dressed in the school colors, green and white, jumpers, blazers, pullover. Our oxfords were tied sturdily all through the winter — replaced by saddle shoes in the spring and the fall. School girls we were in the biology lab and on the hockey field, in the library and in the art studio. School girls reciting Latin declensions, U.S. presidents, the poetry of Emily Dickinson. School girls we were, tutoring younger children.

As we grew older, we became school girls adolescent, with an eye for the macabre, the hypocritical, the absurd. Impossible to manage, we especially maligned the conventional, and that I promise you included the Ellis School's weekly task of memorizing Bible verses. I do not remember exactly how old we were when we were assigned the scripture that we read, "Who can find a virtuous woman, for her price is far above rubies?" But we were old enough that it set our sense of satire loose, our sense of the absurd . . . defiance.

"Who can find a virtuous woman?" We recited it when we were sneak-smoking behind the gymnasium. "Who can find a virtuous woman?" We chanted it as we went over the details of the Saturday dance, how we danced with so and so, and held hands or kissed. "Who can find a virtuous woman?"

We whispered it when we were passing notes to one another in study hall, when we were doing homework together that was meant to be done alone. "Who can find a virtuous woman, who can find a virtuous woman?" It was our refrain, so it is not surprising that as seniors, when we had the "privilege" of designing the class play (meant to reflect our years at the Ellis School), this passage found its way into prominent position. Between each portion, each skit, there was a chorus of school girls, sidling across the stage. "Who can find a virtuous woman, who can find a virtuous woman?"

And in fact this text does strike almost any reader, as an anachronism, a leftover from an ancient culture, valuable perhaps for its historical description of domestic life in Israel of the day, but not valuable for much beyond that. We have come a long, long way in understanding who we are as women since this passage was written. We are equal in God's intention. And we have come too long a way and we know it is we ourselves who decides our virtue — we do — not to let some Hebrew sage tell us.

And there are other problems with this passage. It is choppy. It appears to have no order of thought, no direction. It goes from wool to ships, from night to food, back to clothing, on to wisdom, from bread to fear of the Lord. Why, if any of the Ellis schoolgirls handed in such a poem to our English teacher, she would have written across the top in bold red marks, "not acceptable, no outline, no direction of thought."

How are we to approach such a text? Should we just dismiss it, leave it to the historians? What sense are we to make of it in this worship service? When I have trouble with a biblical text, when I come up against this one, I try to discover as much about the text as is needful, and yes, I was a history major.

This text is the conclusion of the Book of Proverbs which was a sourcebook of materials for the sages, the teachers, of Israel. It is a sourcebook of the development of characters and virtue. It is a how-to book intended for youths even maybe especially youths as incorrigible as we were. It is meant to help young Hebrews, to guide them along the path of wisdom. Has anyone ever given you a book like that? Maybe as a graduation present Marion Wright Edelman's *Letter to My Children* which we gave the seniors.

Proverbs fall into three sections. The first nine chapters introduce us to the context of wisdom, and yes, she is feminine in the Hebrew. Sophia.

The next 19 chapters is a collection of short sayings that we think of as proverbs,

pride goes before the fall

a soft answer turns away wrath

a friend loves at all times.

The last section is four appendix and the last of the four is our text on the virtuous woman.

This poem was probably in circulation in ancient Israel, as an individual piece, given to young women. Then as I send along cards with thoughts, or as you put up posters with our favorite sayings. The poem is an acrostic which may explain why it is so disjointed. Does anyone ever do the acrostics in the Sunday paper — next to the crossword? These take time and smarts and patience, because you need to figure out the formal structure.

The formal structure of this acrostic is the Hebrew's alphabet, the initial letters of the 22 couplets follow the normal order of the Hebrew alphabet.

So then, this poem was chosen by those who put together the Book Of Proverbs, chosen and placed carefully at the end of the Book Of Proverbs, so that the poem might take on greater purpose, a balance for Sophia — wisdom — God. The virtuous woman personifies Sophia and her virtues are valuable for both genders, in both women and men. She is energetic and practical, industrious and shrewd in business. She creates loveliness in all that she touches. She is kind and efficient. She is strong and generous and she fears the Lord.

Who can find a virtuous woman?

Who can find a virtuous person?

57

Who can find a virtuous man?

The passage begins with a rhetorical question to ready us for the description of virtue in Proverbs, so that we might understand what the sages of Israel held as good, true, worthy of report. For some of us, we might agree with the characteristics in this passage. We might respond quite readily, "Yes, yes." Those are characteristics that I cherish." Others might respond, "Mmmm, interesting, but more a curiosity than anything I think about."

At the very least this passage from Proverbs provides for us an occasion to consider what virtues we do value in ourselves and in others . . . what virtues do we value in those we hold dear. I want you to take a moment now to think about what you value in yourself; if virtue seems too old fashioned a word — what characteristic do you value?

Think for a moment, while I tell you about a neighbor who lives alone, and everything he touches turns to loveliness, a vase of black-eyed Susans on the kitchen counter, a strainer full of blueberries in the kitchen sink, a gathering of beach stones on a side table, even his collection of baseball cards is presented in a fashion that is attractive. Our children are mesmerized and he makes time for them. He comes down the hill on his way home from work with a smile and a wave, the kids come running after him tossing a whoosh or a ball. He is patient and generous, he is wise and has a giggle that is infectious, he is a home maker and has a welcoming manner to those in need. These are virtues I value.

The other day we had no water. I called to ask if we could use his bathroom until the plumbers came, and the next thing I knew he was at the kitchen door with a jug of spring water, "I thought you might need this." Who can find a virtuous person, who can find a virtuous woman, who can find a virtuous man. What virtues do you value, in yourself and in those around you?

Another example is a doctor at the Harlem Hospital working with children who have AIDS. She works to prolong the lives and improve the lives of children like Jesus, age nine, whose mother brought him to the doctor after Jesus had been running a fever of 106 for several days. Jesus is limp and withdrawn. The doctor sits down, she will take her time to ask how Jesus is, and how he feels, what he imagines, what he fears. And when Jesus gets to play the doctor for a moment and shine the examining light in her eyes, he even smiles, he even smiles.

"We're smarter now, we're more able to see problems coming and take early action to prevent them," she says. She is a skilled physician, she is modest, an informed researcher and when she is asked why she does what she does she shrugs her shoulders and responds "There is no why. This is my life. I always knew I wanted to work in the inner city. I was always interested in preventative issues." Who can find a virtuous woman . . . for her price is far above rubies? At the end of the day she returns home to her two toddlers, to her husband. Who can find a virtuous woman? What virtues do you value in yourselves and others?

This passage from the end of the Book Of Proverbs provides for us the occasion to consider what virtues we do value in ourselves and those around us. Amen.

Esther: Wise
Woman Of Strength

On a cold and dark March night during my first year at Princeton as assistant dean of the chapel, I left our little home on the edge of the campus to go back to my office. I had a lot of things to accomplish and imagined that the quiet and solitude of the office would be the best place to work. As I approached our office building, Murray-Dodge Hall, I was surprised to see that it was all lit up and I began to hear the sounds of a ruckus. I came through the door and into a lobby to the middle of an astonishing party, a celebration of some sort or another. People were in costume and had noisemakers. There was much cavorting. "Was this Mardi-Gras?" I wondered. "No, Shrove Tuesday had come and gone. What was going on?" I asked myself. "Had the group asked permission of the chapel office?" Working with undergraduates makes one always ready for surprises. It was clear here the surprise for me came in the form of a lot of drinking and rabble-rousing, not usual in Murray-Dodge. Then I saw the rabbi, an abstemious person, clearly a little looped and sidling toward me. "Rabbi!" I explained, "What is going on?" "It's Purim, didn't you know when it was?"

Not only did I not know when Purim was, I did not know what Purim was. But I resolved to find out, for it looked like a lot of fun. I was encouraged to join the celebration, but I went on to my office. It's hard to come to the middle of a party. But I made a promise to myself to learn about Purim, what it was, when it was, why it was, and how long it lasted.

Always one month before Passover, Purim celebrates the story of the Book Of Esther, a tale of twists and turns, ups and downs, ironies and reversals, and a mostly happy ending, at least for the Jews. The characters, especially when compared to the intricate plot, appear one dimensional. King Ahasuerus and Queen Esther, Mordecai and Haman are present to serve the story and the story goes something like this.

After King Ahasuerus, a.k.a. Xerxes, for those who know their history, disposes of his first wife, Vashti, and holds a search for a new queen. Esther enters the harem and gains favor of all who know her and when it is her turn with the king, she is chosen above all the rest to be queen. Esther's guardian is Mordecai, who tells Esther to tell no one about her Judaism and she does not until just the right moment, until she has proven herself indispensable. Mordecai discovers a plot to assassinate the king and reports it to Esther who then saves the king's life. Now she is indispensable. Now she has leverage.

Ahasuerus appoints Haman, above all the princes, and orders all the people to bow down before Haman, Mordecai would not bow down, which is just the excuse Haman was looking for to kill all the Jews. Haman was an inveterate anti-Semite.

In the meantime, the king asks Haman, "What should be done to a man the king delights to honor?" Since Haman imagines it is himself, he answers with great pomp and circumstance, "Let royal robes be brought, a crown on his head set. Let a prince conduct the man on royal horseback all through the square." Only it is Mordecai the king is planning to honor, and has Haman, the enemy who hates him, lead Mordecai through the square, all the time seething and plotting Mordecai's destruction with the rest of the Jews.

Esther understands the evil Haman is planning and invites Haman and the king to a banquet in her quarters. And when the king says to Queen Esther, "What is your petition? It shall be granted, even to half of my kingdom, it shall be fulfilled." Esther tells of the plot to annihilate all the Jews, herself included. When the king asks who would presume to do this, Esther proclaims, "A foe and an enemy! This wicked Haman." So Haman is hung on the gallows prepared for Mordecai and Mordecai is elevated to Haman's position.

This Book Of Esther is a great tale, raucous and ribald as the Purim celebration itself, which I have now attended a number of times with great enthusiasm. During the reading of the Book of Esther which is how the Purim celebration begins, every time Haman's name is mentioned the noisemakers are set off to drown out the evil one. And there are whistles of delight for Mordecai and shouts of joy for Esther and when the Jews are saved and Mordecai is elevated because Esther is so clever and so brave, well, that's when the celebration begins.

We don't need scholars to tell us that the tale of Esther is probably not historically accurate. We can sense on our own that it is a tale, a tale for inspiration, to give people spirit, to help people come to a sense of celebration. The tale of Esther gives us momentum and immense satisfaction. Scholars do tell us though, that the people the storywriter had in mind were the Jews of the second century before the common era, the Jews in the Eastern Diaspora. The tale was written as a model, to help them see how they might attain security and lead productive lives. Esther moves from being a powerless member of a powerless group, a woman in the Jewish Diaspora in Persia, to a queen who has the power to save her people. She uses her intelligence and her beauty, her grit and her grace. She is clever. She is brave. She serves as a model for all who find themselves downtrodden, oppressed, in exile. She serves to inspire all those who need momentum, all those who need hope.

Do you know people who, like Esther, inspire and give hope to those who are downtrodden? Think about those you know while I tell you about Dorothy Day.

I saw her once in Central Park at a rally. By that time she was in her 70s. Her hair was yellow-white and braided over the top, the way she wore it for her whole life. She moved slowly, with a cane, for she suffered from arthritis. But her eyes were filled with wisdom, her face, though deeply wrinkled was filled with faith. Dorothy Day spent her life on the side of the downcast. "It is a strange vocation," she recalled in her memoirs, *The Long Loneliness,* "to love the destitute and dissolute, those people sleeping in doorways, foul with filth in the gutter, dying of hunger or drunkenness, fever and cold." At Saint Joseph's House, hospitality is offered to anyone in need, proving that the works of solace and mercy still comprise the most esteemed of all vocations. Those who arrive are treated with dignity, given a hot meal, a clean room, a sense of self-worth. All her life Dorothy Day lived within the Catholic Church, representing the life of Christ to those who were powerless. She used her intelligence and her beauty, her grit and her grace, on behalf of those who needed her most. Like Esther, she inspires us.

Can you think of others who like Esther and Dorothy Day, give hope to the people, who encourage us along the way?

"Service was as much a part of my upbringing as eating breakfast and going to school. It isn't something you do in your spare time. It was clear that it was the very purpose of life. Helping others had the highest value. There was no black home for the aged in South Carolina when I was growing up so my daddy, who was a minister, started one across the street from us. We all had to get out there and cook and serve. My mother died a few years ago, still running the home for the aged. She was cooking for six old people, all of them younger than she was." Marian Wright Edelman became the first black woman admitted to the bar in Mississippi. She is a graduate of Spelman College and Yale Law School and directed the NAACP Legal Defense Fund in Mississippi and New York. She then founded the Children's Defense Fund, where she serves as its tireless director, lobbying for health care, education and justice for the nation's poorest children, our most defenseless citizens. She uses her intelligence and her beauty, her grit and her grace, on behalf of those who need her most. Like Esther, she inspires us.

"And Mordicai recorded all that has happened and sent letters to the Jews enjoining them that they should keep the 14th day of the month of Adar, and the 15th day, year by year, as the day on which the Jews gained relief from their enemies, and as the month that had been turned for them from sorrow to gladness, from mourning into a holiday; that they should make them days of feasting and gladness, days of sending gifts of food to one another and presents to the poor." Amen.

Lectionary Preaching
After Pentecost

The following index will aid the user of this book in matching the correct Sunday with the appropriate text during Pentecost. All texts in this book are from the series for Lesson One, Common Lectionary. Lutheran and Roman Catholic designations indicate days comparable to Sundays on which Common Lectionary Propers are used.

(Fixed dates do not pertain to Lutheran Lectionary)

Fixed Date Lectionaries *Common and Roman Catholic*	Lutheran Lectionary *Lutheran*
The Day of Pentecost	The Day of Pentecost
The Holy Trinity	The Holy Trinity
May 29-June 4 — Proper 4, Ordinary Time 9	Pentecost 2
June 5-11 — Proper 5, Ordinary Time 10	Pentecost 3
June 12-18 — Proper 6, Ordinary Time 11	Pentecost 4
June 19-25 — Proper 7, Ordinary Time 12	Pentecost 5
June 26-July 2 — Proper 8, Ordinary Time 13	Pentecost 6
July 3-9 — Proper 9, Ordinary Time 14	Pentecost 7
July 10-16 — Proper 10, Ordinary Time 15	Pentecost 8
July 17-23 — Proper 11, Ordinary Time 16	Pentecost 9
July 24-30 — Proper 12, Ordinary Time 17	Pentecost 10
July 31-Aug. 6 — Proper 13, Ordinary Time 18	Pentecost 11
Aug. 7-13 — Proper 14, Ordinary Time 19	Pentecost 12
Aug. 14-20 — Proper 15, Ordinary Time 20	Pentecost 13
Aug. 21-27 — Proper 16, Ordinary Time 21	Pentecost 14
Aug. 28-Sept. 3 — Proper 17, Ordinary Time 22	Pentecost 15
Sept. 4-10 — Proper 18, Ordinary Time 23	Pentecost 16
Sept. 11-17 — Proper 19, Ordinary Time 24	Pentecost 17

Sept. 18-24 — Proper 20, Ordinary Time 25	Pentecost 18
Sept. 25-Oct. 1 — Proper 21, Ordinary Time 26	Pentecost 19
Oct. 2-8 — Proper 22, Ordinary Time 27	Pentecost 20
Oct. 9-15 — Proper 23, Ordinary Time 28	Pentecost 21
Oct. 16-22 — Proper 24, Ordinary Time 29	Pentecost 22
Oct. 23-29 — Proper 25, Ordinary Time 30	Pentecost 23
Oct. 30-Nov. 5 — Proper 26, Ordinary Time 31	Pentecost 24
Nov. 6-12 — Proper 27, Ordinary Time 32	Pentecost 25
Nov. 13-19 — Proper 28, Ordinary Time 33	Pentecost 26 Pentecost 27
Nov. 20-26 — Christ the King	Christ the King

Reformation Day (or last Sunday in October) is October 31 (Common, Lutheran)

All Saints' Day (or first Sunday in November) is November 1 (Common, Lutheran, Roman Catholic)

Books In This Cycle B Series

Gospel Set

Christmas Is A Quantum Leap
Sermons For Advent, Christmas And Epiphany
Glenn Schoonover

From Dusk To Dawn
Sermons For Lent And Easter
C. Michael Mills

The Spirit's Tether
Sermons For Pentecost (First Third)
Leonard H. Budd

Assayings: Theological Faith Testings
Sermons For Pentecost (Middle Third)
Robert L. Salzgeber

Spectators Or Sentinels?
Sermons For Pentecost (Last Third)
Arthur H. Kolsti

First Lesson Set

Why Don't You Send Somebody?
Sermons For Advent, Christmas And Epiphany
Frederick C. Edwards

The Power To Change
Sermons For Lent And Easter
Durwood L. Buchheim

The Way Of The King
Sermons For Pentecost (First Third)
Charles Curley

The Beginning Of Wisdom
Sermons For Pentecost (Middle Third)
Sue Anne Steffey Morrow

Daring To Hope
Sermons For Pentecost (Last Third)
John P. Rossing